fun with folded fabric boxes

- All No-Sew Projects   - Fat-Quarter Friendly   - Elegance in Minutes

Crystal Mills and Arnold Tubis

C&T PUBLISHING

Text © 2007 Crystal Mills and Arnold Tubis

Artwork © 2007 Crystal Mills and C&T Publishing, Inc.

Publisher: Amy Marson

Editorial Director: Gailen Runge

Acquisitions Editor: Jan Grigsby

Editor: Lynn Koolish

Technical Editors: Georgie Gerl and Wendy Mathson

Copyeditor/Proofreader: Wordfirm Inc.

Cover Designer: Kristy Zacharias

Design Director / Book Designer: Christina D. Jarumay

Illustrators: Crystal Mills and Kirstie L. Pettersen

Production Coordinators: Kerry Graham and Kirstie L. Pettersen

Photography by C&T Publishing, Inc., unless otherwise noted

Published by C&T Publishing, Inc., P.O. Box 1456, Lafayette, CA 94549

Library of Congress Cataloging-in-Publication Data

Mills, Crystal Elaine.

Fun with folded fabric boxes : all no-sew projects, fat-quarter friendly, elegance in minutes / Crystal Mills and Arnold Tubis.

p. cm.

ISBN-13: 978-1-57120-399-1 (paper trade : alk. paper)

ISBN-10: 1-57120-399-0 (paper trade : alk. paper)

1. Box making. 2. Origami. 3. Ornamental boxes. 4. Textile fabrics. I. Tubis, Arnold, 1932- II. Title.

TT870.5.M55 2007

736'.982--dc22

2006031543

Printed in China

10 9 8 7 6 5 4 3 2

ACKNOWLEDGMENTS

We'd like to express our thanks to the following individuals:

V'Ann Cornelius, Florence Temko, and Jan Polish of Origami USA for their encouragement and promotion of our single-square origami box designs.

Leon Brown, Ian Harrison (British Origami Society), and Steve Rasmussen (Key Curriculum Press) for their role in initially bringing some of our box designs into book form.

V'Ann Cornelius, Louise Cooper, Boaz Shuval, and Charlene Morrow for their support and helpful suggestions in our previous work on origami boxes.

Charlene Morrow, Jennifer Burge, Connie Culbertson, and Bonnie Larsen for testing the folding diagrams, and for their creative input and suggestions for embellishing our fabric boxes.

The magnificent staff at C&T Publishing, especially Jan Grigsby, Lynn Koolish, Georgie Gerl, and Luke Mulks, for their warm and always friendly support.

The students and teachers in our various workshops at libraries, businesses, museums, and origami and mathematics teacher conventions, for their lively responses and suggestions.

And, finally, our spouses, Charlotte Tubis and George Mills, for their love, understanding, and support throughout our period of collaboration.

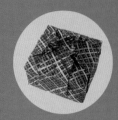

contents

introduction

Although *origami* literally means fold (*ori*) paper (*kami*), you can apply the folding techniques to fabric. The decorative boxes presented in this book are all based on the traditional Japanese *masu*, a folded box that may have been used to measure rice. In this book you will learn some special techniques for folding these boxes from fabric. The fabric is stiffened using a fabric stiffener or bonded to paper or foil. No sewing is involved!

When someone gives a gift in Japan, the gift container or wrapping is often more important than the gift itself. We are sure you will find the same to be true for your gifts when you make the boxes in this book using some of the beautiful quilting fabrics available. You can fold a Self-Closing Box from a single square of fabric, or you can use two fabric squares and fold a separate bottom and a decorative top. Surely you have some fat quarters in your stash that are begging to be used in a project. Perhaps you'll decide to be bold and daring and use fabrics that you might never choose for a quilt. Try mixing and matching fabrics, using one fabric for the box top and a different fabric for the bottom. Almost all the boxes in this book are folded from fat quarters, but you can choose to fold larger boxes from larger fabric pieces.

Before starting your first project, read through the Getting Started chapter and become familiar with the basic materials. Practice stiffening and/or bonding fabric, and find a method that works best for you. If you've had little or no experience with origami or fabric folding, be sure to study the origami folding symbols on page 9, and practice folding one or more of the boxes with paper. Start with the Basic Box (traditional masu), as it forms the basis for all the boxes in the book, then look at the additional folding techniques, which include different ways to finish the inside of the box. With a bit of practice you'll be able to fold a box bottom and lid in very little time.

You'll find that the same box design will look completely different when folded from different fabric. Experiment with bold designs, batiks, stripes, and plaids. You'll often be surprised by the final result. You're sure to have fun creating your own very unique boxes.

getting started

You'll find the information needed for folding all the boxes in this book in the introductory sections. Be sure to read about the materials you'll need and the basic techniques. Become familiar with the origami folding symbols. Before long you'll be ready to fold your first box.

Basic Materials

If you're a quilter, you probably already have most of what you need to begin folding boxes. Once you've decided how you're going to stiffen the fabric, you'll be ready to begin learning the techniques. Whether you're bonding fabric or using a fabric-stiffening product, you'll need the materials listed below.

Paper for Practicing the Folding Steps

Until you become familiar with folding the boxes, you'll want to fold some practice boxes using paper. Leftover wrapping paper or scrapbook paper works well because it has a right and wrong side.

Rotary-Cutting Equipment and Work Surface

Ideally you should use a rotary cutter, ruler, and cutting mat to cut the fabric squares to ensure that your squares are really square. If you use scissors, be sure to cut accurately. You'll also need a large flat surface on which to stiffen and/or bond fabric, and to cut and fold the fabric.

Fabric Markers

Any fabric-marking pencil will work. Be sure to choose a color that you can see on the fabric. Use a light-colored marker on dark fabrics and a dark-colored marker on light fabrics.

Fabric

Good-quality 100% cotton fabric works best. Fat quarters (precut 18″ x 22″ pieces of fabric sold at quilt shops and some fabric stores) are ideal for most boxes. After you gain more experience, you may want to experiment with other fabrics as well, such as silk or rayon.

Cotton fat quarters are ideal fabric choices.

Another product that works well is Michael Miller Fabric Paper. The 12″ squares of fabric have already been stiffened and are ready to fold. You can find Fabric Paper in scrapbooking and craft stores and online (see Resources, page 62).

Fabric paper from Michael Miller

Fabric-Stiffening Materials

To prepare the fabric for folding, you will need to treat it with a stiffening medium. We like to use a product called Stiffy Fabric Stiffener by Plaid Enterprises because it gives consistently good results. Another product we have used is Aleene's Fabric Stiffener and Draping Liquid, which you will need to thin before using. There are also spray-on stiffeners, which are handy if you miss a spot in the fabric-stiffening process (see Resources on page 62). However, we have found it difficult to use the spray to stiffen a large piece of fabric.

Fabric-stiffening materials

Fabric-Bonding Materials

You can bond fabric to paper using Elmer's or Yes! glue, paper-backed fusible web, or spray adhesive. If you use a spray adhesive, be sure to use a cloth face mask and protective goggles, and work in a well-ventilated area. You might also want to use fabric glue for bonding fabric to fabric (see Resources on page 62).

Glues for bonding and decoupage products for finishing

Applicators for Glue or Stiffener

Use a sponge brush to apply glue or stiffener, and a squeegee, an old credit card, or something similar to skim off the excess. Our favorite tool is a hard plastic food scraper.

Applicators for glue or stiffener

Drying Tools

You can use a sweater dryer or hangers and clothespins to dry the wet fabric. We prefer plastic hangers with plastic clips because they don't stick to the fabric like wooden clothespins do.

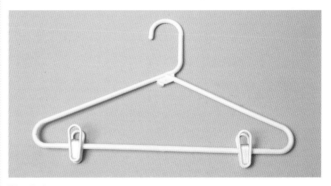

Plastic hanger

Creasing Tools

Try experimenting with a variety of creasing tools to make sharp creases. You can use your fingers, but for most folds you'll probably want a bone folder, a point turner, a Thumble, and/or a miniature iron. Popsicle sticks and tongue depressors also work well as creasers. You should also have a steam iron. Be sure to use a pressing cloth between the iron and the fabric because the stiffener can gum up the bottom of your iron.

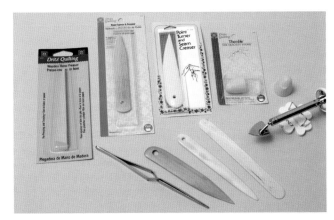
Creasing and shaping tools

Items for Finishing the Box

Thin cardboard inserts help strengthen the sides and maintain the shape of a finished box, making it very square. The inserts won't be visible in your finished box, so it doesn't matter what material you use. Cereal boxes are a good weight. You can also use fast2fuse Double-Sided Fusible Stiff Interfacing (see Resources on page 62). Depending on the materials you use, two of the sides may be stiff enough (because of the multiple layers) so that additional stiffeners won't be necessary. To give your box a professional finished look and prevent it from losing its shape in humid weather, apply a coat or two of Mod Podge or another decoupage finish.

Basic Techniques

Preparing the Fabric

A fat quarter is a good size for most of the boxes. It's not necessary to prewash the fabric. Stiffen the whole fat quarter, and cut it to size after stiffening.

> ● tip
>
> *Plan to stiffen a number of fat quarters at a time. Approximately ten to twelve fat quarters can be stiffened with one 16-ounce bottle of Stiffy. This will give you plenty of fabric that is ready to fold, and you only need to clean up once.*

1. Lay the fabric on a flat surface, and use a sponge brush to apply the stiffener to one side of the fabric. (If you use Aleene's Fabric Stiffener, be sure to thin it first. It should be the consistency of milk.)

2. Turn the fabric over and check to make sure the stiffener has saturated the fabric. If necessary, apply more stiffener.

3. Use a squeegee, plastic scraper, or something similar to skim off the excess stiffener and smooth out the fabric. Be sure to clean your work space and tools with soap and water.

4. Lay the treated fabric on a sweater dryer or hang it up to dry using a hanger and clothespins. It usually takes about 1½ to 2 hours to dry. Drying, especially if the fabric is placed outside on a sunny day, occurs rapidly. Do not put the wet fabric into a clothes dryer.

Drying the fabric

> ● tip
>
> *If the sun isn't shining and you want to dry the fabric quickly, use a hair dryer.*

Don't worry if wrinkles or waves develop in the fabric. Once the fabric is dry, you can iron it with a steam iron to smooth it out. Be sure to place a pressing cloth over the fabric so that residue from the fabric stiffener doesn't get on the bottom of your iron.

Bonding Fabric to a Backing

We think that using fabric stiffener is the best way to prepare cotton fabric for folding. However, if you want to experiment with other kinds of fabric, such as silk or rayon, you can try bonding it to paper. There are several methods you can use for the bonding.

Use a sponge brush to spread a thin layer of regular craft glue such as Elmer's or Yes! Spread the glue evenly on the backing, diluting it with warm water if necessary. Skim off any excess. Experiment with the thickness of the glue layer. If the layer is too thick, the bonded fabric may become too stiff and brittle to fold. Use a rolling pin and/or a warm iron to eliminate bubbles and smooth out the bonding.

You can also use a paper-backed fusible web, such as Heat 'n' Bond, WonderUnder, or Stitch Witchery, which is sold in fabric stores. Another alternative is a spray adhesive. When using either of these products, be sure to follow the manufacturer's instructions.

Working with Stiffened or Bonded Fabric

Working with stiffened fabric or fabric bonded to paper is similar to working with ordinary paper. In particular, you can make sharp creases by finger-pressing or using a bone folder or even a smoothed-edged piece of wood such as a Popsicle stick or tongue depressor. You might want to use a miniature iron to help sharpen some of the creases. Ironing initially softens the fabric, but the fabric rapidly regains stiffness again when it cools.

Make sharp creases.

Finishing the Box

Stiffening the Sides of the Box

You may want to stiffen the sides of your box and/or the lid. If so, you can unfold the box and insert pieces of thin cardboard between the layers of fabric that form the sides. You can also use fast2fuse; the interfacing works well on the sides where there are only two layers of fabric. The other two sides of the box are already stiffer due to the multiple layers formed when folding the box, so you may not need additional stiffening on those sides.

Applying a Finishing Coat

Use a sponge brush to apply one or two coats of Mod Podge or a similar decoupage product (see Resources on page 62) to give your box a lasting finish. You can use a matte, semigloss, or glossy finish. Mod Podge also comes in a sparkle finish. This technique works particularly well in humid climates, where the inside edges of stiffened fabric tend to curl over time.

Designing Boxes of Desired Dimensions

With some experimenting, you'll soon be folding boxes of any size. At the end of each chapter you'll find a chart listing a variety of box and lid sizes, and the size of the fabric square you need to start with. At the back of the book are formulas you can use to create any of the boxes and lids in this book in any size you like.

Because of variations in the thickness of the fabric, the amount of stiffening, the backing, and the bonding medium, the tables list approximate finished dimensions. For this reason, you'll find the techniques for producing snugly fitting box bottom and lid combinations starting on page 13 very useful, and you'll be able to create any size box.

Origami Folding Symbols

Become familiar with these folding symbols, and refer to them when you're learning to fold a new box.

 tip

Notice the color and type of line for each type of fold.

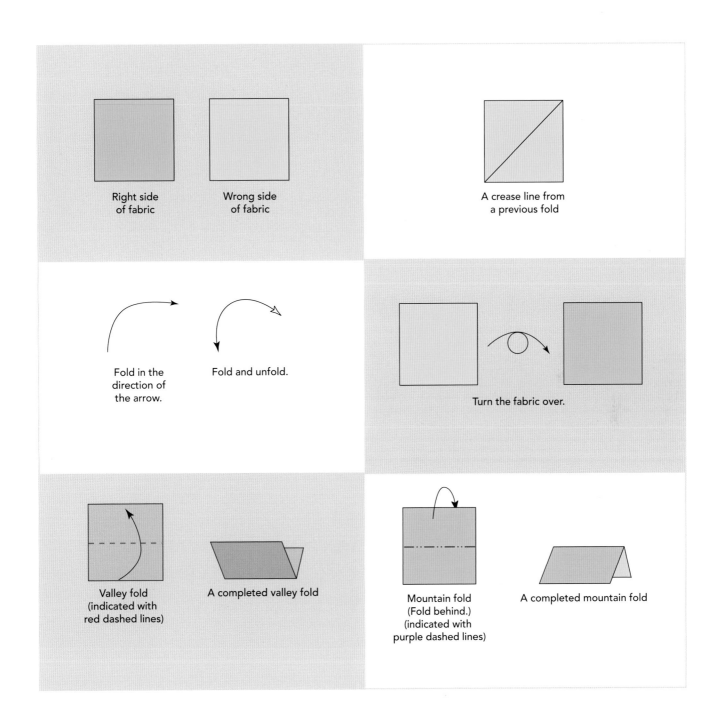

Right side of fabric

Wrong side of fabric

A crease line from a previous fold

Fold in the direction of the arrow.

Fold and unfold.

Turn the fabric over.

Valley fold (indicated with red dashed lines)

A completed valley fold

Mountain fold (Fold behind.) (indicated with purple dashed lines)

A completed mountain fold

basic box
(Traditional Japanese Masu)

Preparing the Fabric

Follow the directions on pages 7–8, and stiffen your fabric using fabric stiffener or by bonding it to paper or interfacing.

Cutting the Fabric

The finished dimensions of your box will depend on the size of the fabric square you start with. The height of a standard box is half the edge length of the bottom square. You can use the table below to determine the approximate dimensions of a finished standard-height box for several different starting square sizes. The measurements of your box may differ due to the stiffness of your fabric and the accuracy of your folding.

Starting Square	Finished Height	Finished Size
$17'' \times 17''$	$3''$	$6'' \times 6''$
$15'' \times 15''$	$2^5/_8''$	$5^1/_4'' \times 5^1/_4''$
$12'' \times 12''$	$2^1/_8''$	$4^1/_4'' \times 4^1/_4''$
$11^1/_4'' \times 11^1/_4''$	$2''$	$4'' \times 4''$

To learn how to vary the height of any of the boxes you fold in this book, see page 62.

In this chapter you'll learn to fold a basic box. You'll also learn some basic techniques for making lids. You can use this box by itself or as the bottom for a decorative lid.

What You'll Need

Fabric

One fat quarter of fabric (or paper if you're just practicing)

Basic materials (See pages 5–7.)

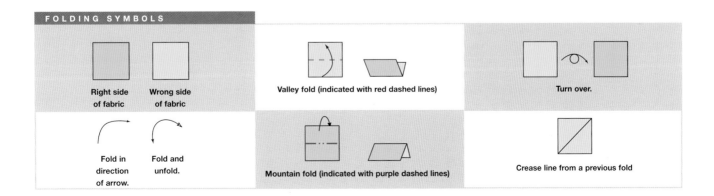

FOLDING SYMBOLS

Right side of fabric — Wrong side of fabric

Fold in direction of arrow. — Fold and unfold.

Valley fold (indicated with red dashed lines)

Mountain fold (indicated with purple dashed lines)

Turn over.

Crease line from a previous fold

Folding the Basic Box

This box (masu) is a traditional origami model that forms the basis for all the other boxes in this book. Before you start folding, refer back to the origami folding symbols on page 11. Then follow the diagrams below to fold a box.

Step 1: Start with the wrong side of the fabric square facing up. Fold and unfold the horizontal and vertical valley folds.

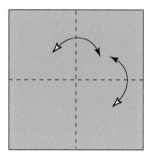

Step 2: Bring each corner to the center, and crease.

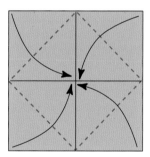

Step 3: Fold each edge to the center, and unfold. Make sure the folds are parallel to the outside edge.

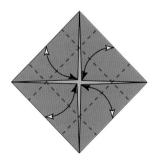

Step 4: Unfold an opposite pair of triangles.

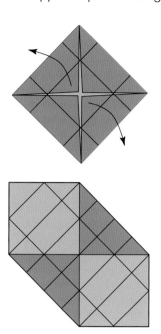

Step 5: Form 2 sides of the box by refolding the indicated valleys (red dashed lines) so the sides stand up.

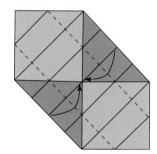

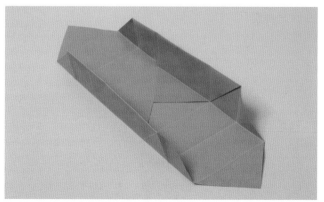

Two sides of the box folded up

Step 6: Push in as indicated, and fold the other 2 sides up and over to form the box.

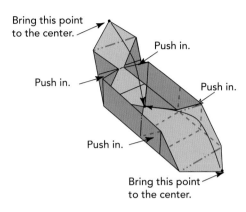

Bring this point to the center.

Push in.

Push in.

Push in.

Push in.

Push in.

Bring this point to the center.

Three sides of the box folded

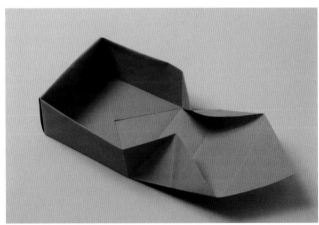

The Basic Box or box bottom

Folding Snugly Fitting Box Bottoms and Lids

It is usually easier to first fold a box bottom and then fold a lid that will snugly fit the bottom. Here are two techniques for fitting a lid to a box bottom. Try both and decide which method you prefer.

Rather than making a separate lid, you can make any of the boxes in this book self-closing. See pages 22–23 for instructions.

Folding a Snugly Fitting Lid— Technique 1

Step 1: First, fold the box bottom.

Step 2: With another piece of stiffened fabric, complete Steps 1 and 2 of Folding the Basic Box (page 12).

Step 3: Place the box bottom in the corner of the flattened lid, aligned with the top and side edges.

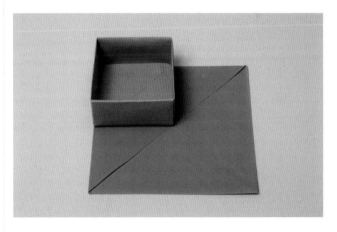

Step 4: Fold the bottom edge of the flattened lid to the bottom edge of the box bottom, and crease.

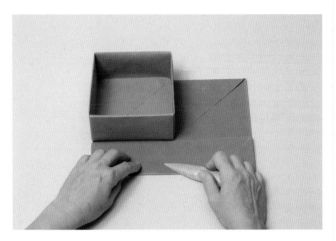

Step 5: Open the fold, and fold the side edge of the flattened lid to the side edge of the box bottom, and crease. Open the fold.

Step 6: Move the box bottom to another corner, and follow Steps 4 and 5 for the other sides, until all 4 sides are creased.

Step 7: Follow Steps 4 through 6 of Folding the Basic Box (pages 12–13) to complete the lid.

In fitting a box lid to a bottom, initially make very light creases before making a final set of sharp creases. If the lid is a little too snug or loose, unfold to Step 2 of the box folds. Use a pressing cloth and a steam iron and press the flattened lid. Once the fabric cools you can refold the lid.

Folding a Snugly Fitting Lid— Technique 2

Step 1: Complete Steps 1 and 2 of Technique 1 (page 13).

Step 2: Place the box bottom on the flattened lid so that each corner lies on one of the diagonal lines of the lid. Be sure the box bottom is centered on the lid. Use a fabric marker to place a mark about 1/8″ away from one edge of the box bottom.

Step 3: Fold on the mark you made in Step 2 to form one side of the lid.

Step 4: Use the intersection of the fold line and the diagonal to determine the fold line for the second side.

Step 5: Continue folding the other sides in the same manner.

Step 6: Follow Steps 4 through 6 of Folding the Basic Box (pages 12–13) to complete the lid.

Varying the Height of the Box

The folds you make in Step 3 (page 12) determine the height of the box. Steps 4, 5, and 6 are the same for boxes of any height. As the height of a box decreases, the edge length of the square bottom increases.

■ To make a shallower box, don't fold the edges all the way to the center.

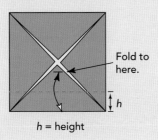

h = height

■ To make a deeper box, fold the edges past the center.

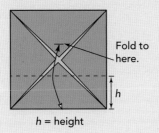

h = height

Once you have folded one edge, be sure to fold the other edges so that all 4 sides of the box will be the same height. To do this, look at where the first fold crosses the diagonal of the square. The point of intersection determines the depth of the next fold.

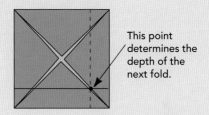

This point determines the depth of the next fold.

Continue folding and unfolding until you have completed all 4 folds. Then follow Steps 4 through 6 of Folding the Basic Box (pages 12–13).

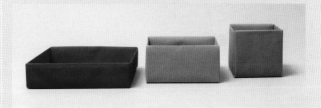

All 3 boxes were folded from the same size fabric square.

The table below gives approximate dimensions for several nonstandard-height boxes. See page 62 for formulas to calculate other sizes.

Starting Square	Finished Height	Finished Size
17″ × 17″	$3\frac{1}{2}$″	5″ × 5″
15″ × 15″	2″	$6\frac{1}{2}$″ × $6\frac{1}{2}$″
$12\frac{3}{4}$″ × $12\frac{3}{4}$″	3″	3″ × 3″

Other Options for the Basic Box

A cubic box makes just the right size holder for tea bags.

Make a lid for your box bottom. A fat quarter of wide striped fabric and a button make a very special box.

A Self-Closing Box (see page 22–23) can hold a special gift. The fabric used for this box is heavier cotton that was bonded to paper.

A shallow box makes a nice napkin holder. A small cubic box holds toothpicks.

additional folding
techniques

Basic Folds

Be sure to practice these basic folding sequences with paper. You'll use them when folding several of the decorative lids or boxes.

Folding a Preliminary Base

Step 1: With the right side of the fabric square facing up, fold and then unfold the valley creases. Turn the fabric over.

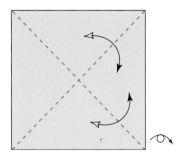

Step 2: With the wrong side facing up, fold the square in half and unfold as shown to make vertical and horizontal creases. Turn the fabric over.

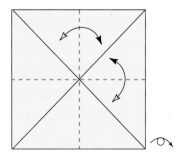

 tip

As you are folding, look at the next step to see what the piece should look like when the current step is completed.

Step 3: Make the indicated mountain fold.

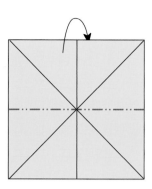

Step 4: Grasp both sides of the top mountain fold and bring your hands down toward each other. As you do this, two additional mountain folds and two valley folds will be formed and the model will collapse into a smaller multilayered square.

Bring your hands down toward each other.

A completed Preliminary Base

Sink Fold

Step 1: Fold a Preliminary Base (see page 18).

Step 2: Fold the top corner down toward the front, and then unfold. Refold the same fold to the back. The depth of the fold (*d*) will vary depending on the size of your box.

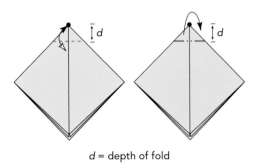

d = depth of fold

Step 3: Unfold the fabric completely. With the fabric right side up, refold the indicated mountains and valleys. Notice that the edges of the small square in the center are all mountain folds. The diagonals of this square are valleys. If you make the folds carefully, the folds in the next step will just fall into place.

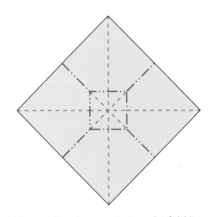

Valley (red) and mountain (purple) fold lines

Step 4: Refold the Preliminary Base while pushing down on the center point. The center square should automatically collapse. If it doesn't, check the folds you made in Step 3.

See the "sink" in the middle.

A completed Sink Fold

Finishing the Inside of the Box

In origami, you usually don't use glue; however, you may want to glue down the loose tabs on the inside of the box because eventually they may curl. Or you can fold either a tab-lock insert or a side-to-side divider to finish the inside of the box (see next page).

The tab-lock insert (page 20) will hold the triangular-shaped tabs in place, although you may still want to use glue to hold the tabs and the tab-lock insert in place. A decoupage finish will also help keep the flaps and the insert in place.

The side-to-side divider (page 21) will divide the box into compartments that are especially useful for storing small things.

Box with tab-lock insert

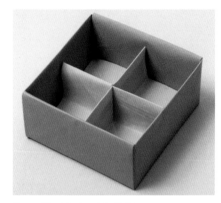

Box with side-to-side divider

Folding the Tab-Lock Insert

To fold a tab-lock insert, start with 2 identical squares of stiffened fabric. For an insert that is easy to attach, start with squares whose edge lengths are equal to the length of the bottom of the box. For a tab-lock that completely fills the bottom of the box, start with 2 squares that have edge lengths that are twice the edge length of the bottom. (For example, if the box bottom is 4″ × 4″, start with 2 squares that are 8″ × 8″.) Fold both squares following Steps 1 through 3.

Step 1: Fold one edge of the square toward the center. Make sure the fold is parallel to the outside edge, and crease. The distance x is arbitrary but should be about ¼ the width of the square. Repeat with the second square.

x is approximately ¼ the width measurement. Repeat with the second square.

Step 2: Fold over the opposite edge so that it meets the first edge and is parallel to the outside edge. Crease. Repeat with the second square.

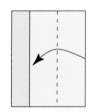

Repeat with the second square.

Step 3: Fold the top down about ¼ the side-edge length and the bottom up so that the top and bottom edges meet. Make the folds parallel to the outside edge. Crease. Repeat with the second square.

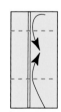

Repeat with the second square.

Step 4: Rotate one piece 90°, and turn it over. Insert the flaps of one piece into the pockets of the other piece.

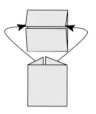

Now you have a tab-lock insert—a square with a pocket on each side.

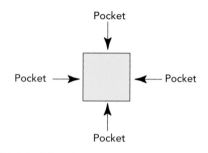

A tab-lock insert

Tuck each triangular tab of the box into one of the pockets of the tab-lock insert.

Folding the Side-to-Side Divider Insert

To determine how large the original square for the insert should be, double the height that you want the divider to be, add the edge length of the box bottom, and then add ¼″. (For example, if the divider is to be 3″ high and the edge length of the box bottom is 6″, the edge length of the starting square for the divider should be: 3″ + 3″ + 6″ + ¼″ = 12¼″

The bottom of your insert may be slightly larger than the bottom of the box, but you can trim it to size (see tip on page 22).

Step 1: With the wrong side of the square facing up, fold and unfold the indicated valleys. Then turn the fabric over.

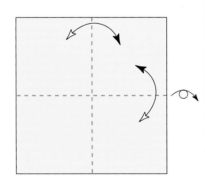

Step 2: Fold and unfold the indicated valleys.

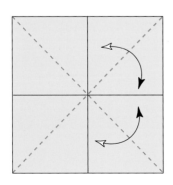

Step 3: Refold the mountains and valleys as shown so that the center point E is below points A, B, C, and D. Turn the square wrong side up and bring point A to point D and point B to point C. The square should collapse into a multilayered triangle with point E at the bottom.

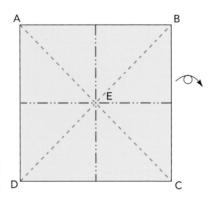

Step 4: Check to make sure the wrong side of the fabric is on the outside. Fold the tip up. The value of *h* will determine the height of the divider.

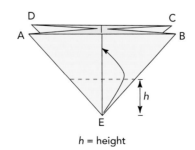

h = height

Step 5: Fold and unfold the indicated valleys on the front 2 layers **and** the back 2 layers.

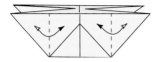

Step 6: Bring the front layer forward and the back layer back until they both lie on a horizontal surface.

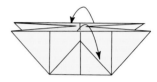

Step 7: Fold the indicated valleys and mountain. As you make the folds, you will be forming 2 divider walls that are perpendicular to each other.

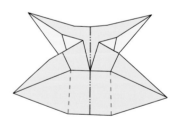

Completed side-to-side divider

For stability, insert 1 long and 2 short thin cardboard rectangles inside the walls of the divider.

Cardboard inserts

You can fine-tune the fit of the insert by trimming the top of the partially folded insert (shown in Step 3). To get the correct size, line up the folded edge of the insert with the center of the folded box (see bottom photo).

Folding a Self-Closing Box

With just a few extra folds, you can make any **standard-height box** in this book self-closing.

Note: *If you make a Self-Closing Box from one of the decorative lids in this book, the opening of the box will be on the bottom.*

Step 1: Complete all the steps for folding the Basic Box (pages 12–13). Then completely unfold it.

Step 2: With the wrong side up, make the indicated valley folds, and refold the 4 short mountain folds as shown.

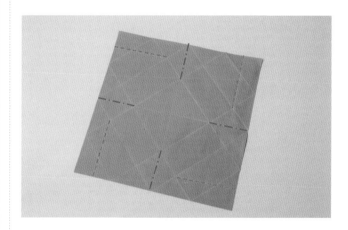

Step 3: Paper clip the valleys to form the tabs.

Step 4: Re-form the box by pushing the corners in and standing the sides and tabs up vertically.

Step 5: Fold the right tab down.

Step 6: Fold the top tab down on top of the right tab.

Step 7: Fold the left tab down.

Step 8: Fold the bottom tab down, and tuck it under the tab on the right to close and lock the box. Remove the paper clips.

Self-Closing Box

banded box

Now that you've mastered the Basic Box and lid, you're ready to fold your first decorative lid or closed box. The Banded Box has ribbonlike bands with a square knot in the center of the top.

What You'll Need

Fabric

- For a Self-Closing Box: 1 fat quarter of stiffened fabric **OR**

- For a box and a lid: 2 fat quarters of stiffened fabric

- For a side-to-side divider for the box bottom: 1 fat quarter of stiffened fabric

Basic materials (See pages 5–7.)

Cutting the Fabric Squares

- For a Self-Closing Box: Cut 1 square 16″ × 16″ **OR**

- For a box and a lid: Cut 2 squares 16″ × 16″.

- For a tab-lock insert: Cut 2 smaller squares out of leftover fabric **OR**

- For a side-to-side divider: Cut 1 square 12″ × 12″.

Folding the Box Bottom

Fold a standard-height Basic Box (see pages 12–13). Finish the bottom with a tab-lock insert or a side-to-side divider (see pages 19–22).

Folding a Lid or a Closed Box

Step 1: Complete Steps 1 and 2 of the Basic Box (see page 12). Unfold.

Step 2: Fold a Preliminary Base (see page 18).

Step 3: Be sure the folded edges are at the top and the cut edges are at the bottom. Fold the top corner down 1¾″ or the distance (d) desired. Unfold.

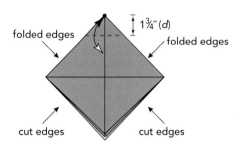

folded edges — folded edges
1¾″ (d)
cut edges — cut edges

d = depth of fold

You can change the depth of the fold (d) to make the bands wider or narrower. The width of the band will be the same as the depth of the fold (d).

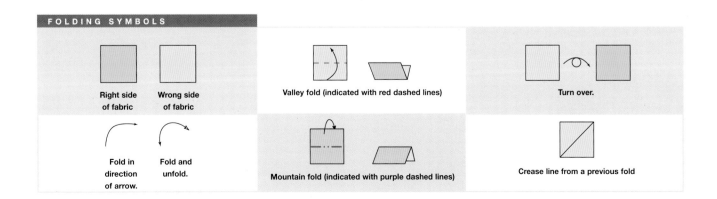

FOLDING SYMBOLS

Right side of fabric | Wrong side of fabric

Valley fold (indicated with red dashed lines)

Turn over.

Fold in direction of arrow. | Fold and unfold.

Mountain fold (indicated with purple dashed lines)

Crease line from a previous fold

Step 4: Fold and unfold the front 2 layers of fabric as shown. Turn the piece over, and make the same folds on the back 2 layers.

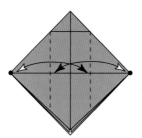

Step 5: Place each fold line from Step 4 on the centerline and crease. Turn the piece over, and repeat these folds on the other side.

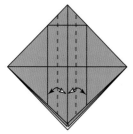

Step 6: Open completely, and valley fold each corner as shown.

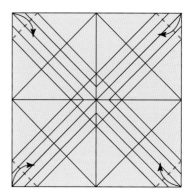

Step 7: Refold the mountain folds as shown. Bring each mountain crease line to one of the center diagonals and crease.

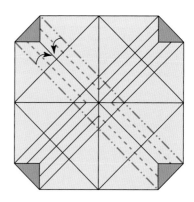

Step 8: Bring each mountain crease line to the other center diagonal and crease through all the layers.

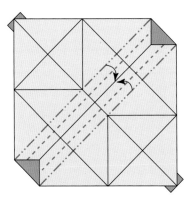

Step 9: To fold a Self-Closing Box, follow the directions for the Self-Closing Box on pages 22–23, keeping the Banded Box folds in place. Otherwise, follow the procedure for folding snugly fitting lids on pages 13–14.

Step 10: To lock the inside tabs, tuck the ends underneath each other, going in a clockwise or counterclockwise direction.

Size Options for Banded Box Lids and Box Bottoms

	Starting Square (*l*)	Finished Height (*h*)	Finished Size (*s*)	Depth of Fold (*d*)
Lid	$17\frac{1}{4}'' \times 17\frac{1}{4}''$	$1\frac{1}{4}''$	$6\frac{1}{4}'' \times 6\frac{1}{4}''$	$1\frac{3}{4}''$
Box Bottom	$14'' \times 14''$	$2''$	$6'' \times 6''$	
Lid	$16'' \times 16''$	$1''$	$5\frac{7}{8}'' \times 5\frac{7}{8}''$	$1\frac{3}{4}''$
Box Bottom	$16'' \times 16''$	$2\frac{7}{8}''$	$5\frac{5}{8}'' \times 5\frac{5}{8}''$	
Lid	$15\frac{1}{2}'' \times 15\frac{1}{2}''$	$1\frac{1}{4}''$	$4\frac{3}{4}'' \times 4\frac{3}{4}''$	$1\frac{7}{8}''$
Box Bottom	$15\frac{1}{2}'' \times 15\frac{1}{2}''$	$3\frac{3}{8}''$	$4\frac{1}{4}'' \times 4\frac{1}{4}''$	
Lid	$14'' \times 14''$	$1\frac{1}{8}''$	$4\frac{3}{4}'' \times 4\frac{3}{4}''$	$1\frac{1}{2}''$
Box Bottom	$12\frac{1}{2}'' \times 12\frac{1}{2}''$	$2\frac{1}{8}''$	$4\frac{1}{2}'' \times 4\frac{1}{2}''$	
Lid	$12'' \times 12''$	$1\frac{1}{4}''$	$4\frac{1}{2}'' \times 4\frac{1}{2}''$	$\frac{3}{4}''$
Box Bottom	$12'' \times 12''$	$2\frac{1}{8}''$	$4\frac{1}{4}'' \times 4\frac{1}{4}''$	

Other Options

Bright and bold fabrics
make a striking box with
a tall Basic Box bottom.
The flower button makes
it extra special.

A plaid and a print make
an interesting combination.
Notice how the plaid looks
like it's on the diagonal
when folded into a box.

Make a shamrock box
for St. Patrick's Day, and
fill it with lucky charms.
This one has a shallow
box bottom.

This box is folded from
painted silk that has
been bonded to paper.

flower box I

T his box has a decorative flower fold on its top. Use a pretty flowered fabric or any other fabric of your choice.

What You'll Need

Fabric

- For a Self-Closing Box: 1 fat quarter of stiffened fabric **OR**

- For a box and a lid: 2 fat quarters of stiffened fabric

- For a side-to-side divider for the box bottom: 1 fat quarter of stiffened fabric

Basic materials (See pages 5–7.)

Cutting the Fabric Squares

- For a Self-Closing Box: Cut 1 square 17″ × 17″ **OR**

- For a box and a lid: Cut 2 squares 17″ × 17″.

- For a tab-lock insert: Cut 2 smaller squares out of leftover fabric **OR**

- For a side-to-side divider: Cut 1 square 12½″ × 12½″.

Folding the Box Bottom

Fold a standard-height Basic Box (see pages 12–13). Finish the bottom with a tab-lock insert or a side-to-side divider (see pages 19–22).

Folding a Lid or a Closed Box

Step 1: Fold a Preliminary Base (see page 18).

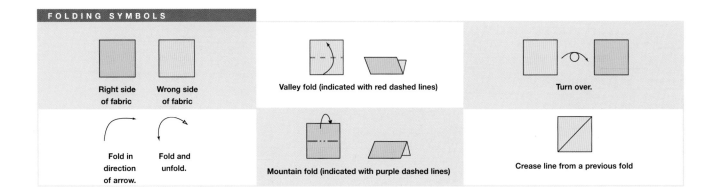

FOLDING SYMBOLS		
Right side of fabric Wrong side of fabric	Valley fold (indicated with red dashed lines)	Turn over.
Fold in direction of arrow. Fold and unfold.	Mountain fold (indicated with purple dashed lines)	Crease line from a previous fold

Step 2: Be sure the folded edges are at the top and the cut edges are at the bottom. Fold the top corner down 1¾″ or the distance (*d*) desired. Unfold.

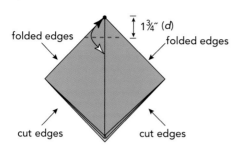

folded edges   1¾″ (*d*)   folded edges

cut edges   cut edges

d = depth of fold

*Making a deeper fold (increasing d) will **increase** the width of the decorative bands and **decrease** the depth of the lid.*

Step 3: Make a Sink Fold (see page 19).

Sink

Step 4: Make the indicated valley folds on the front 2 layers, making sure the top fold aligns with the centerline. Turn the fabric over and make the same 2 folds on the back layers.

Step 5: Rotate the fabric 180° so that the unfolded edges are at the top. Pull apart the layers and flatten the fabric. As you pull apart the layers, a small, multi-layered square knot will form on the underside.

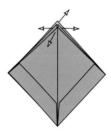

The square knot on the underside is often called a lover's knot.

Step 6: With the fabric right side up, fold each rib in half lengthwise.

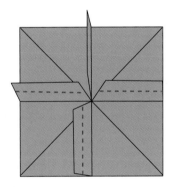

Step 7: Stand each rib up vertically and open the pocket near the center. Then flatten the rib from the outside edge toward the center.

Flattened rib

• tip

Try inserting a long, blunt tool, such as a chopstick, into the rib to help when flattening. The blunt end of a bone or bamboo folder can be used to help shape the end of each rib near the center.

• tip

To make it easier to flatten the ribs in the next step, fold in both directions when making the lengthwise crease.

Center detail after ribs are flattened

Step 8: To fold a Self-Closing Box, follow the directions for the Self-Closing Box on pages 22–23, keeping the Flower Box folds in place. Otherwise, follow the procedure for folding snugly fitting lids on pages 13–14.

To make the corners of the lid less bulky, cut off the 8 small triangular tabs, as indicated in the diagram.

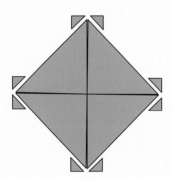

Step 9: Lock the inside flaps by tucking them under the center square or make a tab-lock (pages 19–20) insert if you want a different color at the inside center of the lid.

Step 10: Turn the lid over and shape the flower on the top.

Size Options for Flower Box I Lids and Box Bottoms

	Starting Square (*l*)	Finished Height (*h*)	Finished Size (*s*)	Depth of Fold (*d*)
Lid	$11^5/8'' \times 11^5/8''$	$1^1/8''$	$4^5/8'' \times 4^5/8''$	$1^3/8''$
Box Bottom	$12'' \times 12''$	$2^1/8''$	$4^1/4'' \times 4^1/4''$	
Lid	$12'' \times 12''$	$1^3/8''$	$4^1/4'' \times 4^1/4''$	$1^3/8''$
Box Bottom	$11^1/4'' \times 11^1/4''$	$2''$	$4'' \times 4''$	
Lid	$16'' \times 16''$	$1^3/8''$	$6^1/4'' \times 6^1/4''$	$2^3/8''$
Box Bottom	$17'' \times 17''$	$3''$	$6'' \times 6''$	
Lid	$17'' \times 17''$	$2''$	$6^1/2'' \times 6^1/2''$	$1^1/2''$
Box Bottom	$17'' \times 17''$	$3''$	$6'' \times 6''$	

Other Options

A pretty flowered print for the lid and a contrasting one for the bottom make an attractive standard-height box.

The stars in this print are dimensional and multicolored. They almost look like they would glow in the dark.

Cutout animals glued to pieces of foam add interest to this box.

A multicolored batik makes a very ethnic-looking box.

flower box II

Cutting the Fabric Squares

- For a Self-Closing Box: Cut 1 square 15″ × 15″ **OR**

- For a box and a lid: Cut 2 squares 15″ × 15″.

- For a tab-lock insert: Cut 2 smaller squares out of leftover fabric **OR**

- For a side-to-side divider: Cut 1 square 11″ × 11″.

Folding the Box Bottom

Fold a standard-height Basic Box (see pages 12–13). Finish the bottom with a tab-lock insert or a side-to-side divider (see pages 19–22).

Folding a Lid or a Closed Box

Step 1: Complete Steps 1 and 2 of the Basic Box (see page 12). Unfold.

Step 2: Complete Steps 1 through 5 of the Banded Box (see page 25–26). Fold the top corner down 1½″ (d).

Are you ready to try a more challenging box? The "flower" on the top of this box is nestled under triangular petals.

What You'll Need

Fabric

- For a Self-Closing Box: 1 fat quarter of stiffened fabric **OR**

- For a box and a lid: 2 fat quarters of stiffened fabric

- For a side-to-side divider for the box bottom: 1 fat quarter of stiffened fabric

Basic materials (See pages 5–7.)

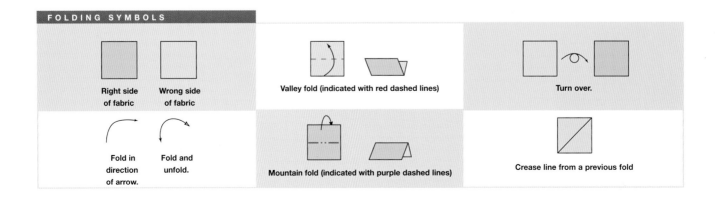

FOLDING SYMBOLS

Right side of fabric	Wrong side of fabric	Valley fold (indicated with red dashed lines)	Turn over.
Fold in direction of arrow.	Fold and unfold.	Mountain fold (indicated with purple dashed lines)	Crease line from a previous fold

Step 3: Make a Sink Fold (see page 19).

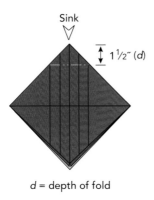

d = depth of fold

Step 4: Make the indicated valley folds on the front 2 layers, making sure the top fold aligns with the centerline. Turn the fabric over and make the same 2 folds on the back layers.

Step 5: Rotate the fabric 180° so that the unfolded edges are at the top. Pull apart the layers and flatten the fabric. As you pull apart the layers, a small square knot will be formed on the underside.

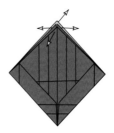

Step 6: Valley fold each corner as indicated. Turn the fabric over so the right side is facing up. Stand the ribs up.

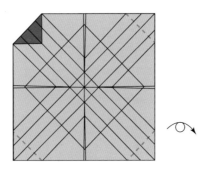

Step 7: Instead of flattening each rib as you did for Flower Box I, you will be flattening each rib into a large triangular section (rib).

Open the pocket at the center, and stand a rib up vertically so that the rib end at the edge is directly above the end at the center. As you stand up the rib, make 2 new creases on either side of the rib. Refold the other short creases that form sides of the small triangles on the flattened part of the rib.

Step 8: Refer to the photo below, and carefully note the valley and mountain folds along existing crease lines. (You may need to reverse some folds to make the mountains and valleys.) Gently push up from underneath to form a triangular rib. Then flatten the rib.

Form the triangular rib.

After you fold all the ribs, your fabric square should look like this.

Step 9: To fold a Self-Closing Box, follow the directions for the Self-Closing Box on pages 22–23, keeping the Flower Box folds in place. Otherwise, follow the procedure for folding snugly fitting lids on pages 13–14.

Step 10: To finish the inside, tuck the corners of each tab into the adjacent pocket. As an alternative, lock the tabs with a tab-lock insert (pages 19–20) if you want a different color on the inside of the lid.

Step 11: Turn the lid over and shape the flower on the top.

 tip

To obtain an interesting curled-petal form of the flower, use tweezers to twist the petal flaps toward the corners of the lid top and then release them.

Size Options for Flower Box II Lids and Box Bottoms

	Starting Square (l)	Finished Height (h)	Finished Size (s)	Depth of Fold (d)
Lid	$15\frac{1}{2}'' \times 15\frac{1}{2}''$	$1\frac{3}{8}''$	$5\frac{1}{4}'' \times 5\frac{1}{4}''$	$1\frac{1}{2}''$
Box Bottom	$17'' \times 17''$	$3\frac{1}{2}''$	$5'' \times 5''$	
Lid	$16\frac{1}{4}'' \times 16\frac{1}{4}''$	$1\frac{1}{8}''$	$6\frac{1}{4}'' \times 6\frac{1}{4}''$	$1\frac{1}{2}''$
Box Bottom	$16\frac{1}{4}'' \times 16\frac{1}{4}''$	$2\frac{7}{8}''$	$5\frac{3}{4}'' \times 5\frac{3}{4}''$	
Lid	$15'' \times 15''$	$1''$	$5\frac{5}{8}'' \times 5\frac{5}{8}''$	$1\frac{1}{2}''$
Box Bottom	$15'' \times 15''$	$2\frac{5}{8}''$	$5\frac{1}{4}'' \times 5\frac{1}{4}''$	
Lid	$13'' \times 13''$	$1\frac{1}{8}''$	$5'' \times 5''$	$1''$
Box Bottom	$13'' \times 13''$	$2\frac{1}{4}''$	$4\frac{3}{4}'' \times 4\frac{3}{4}''$	

Other Options

You can have fun shaping the flower on the top of this box. Notice how different the boxes can look. Two of the boxes have flowers hidden under triangular petals. The flower covers the top of the box in others.

Painted silk bonded to paper gives this box an especially elegant appearance.

The swirls in the fabric create a beautiful flower on this tall box.

The flower is in full bloom on this box folded from batik fabric.

Mod Podge helps the flower on the top of this pink and black box hold its shape.

victorian box

If you've folded Flower Box II, then this box will be a snap. Just make a little change in one of the final steps of the folding sequence.

What You'll Need

Fabric

- For a Self-Closing Box: 1 fat quarter of stiffened fabric **OR**

- For a box and a lid: 2 fat quarters of stiffened fabric

- For a side-to-side divider for the box bottom: 1 fat quarter of stiffened fabric

Basic materials (See pages 5–7.)

Cutting the Fabric Squares

- For a Self-Closing Box: Cut 1 square 17″ × 17″ **OR**

- For a box and a lid: Cut 2 squares 17″ × 17″.

- For a tab-lock insert: Cut 2 smaller squares out of leftover fabric **OR**

- For a side-to-side divider: Cut 1 square 12″ × 12″.

Folding the Box Bottom

Fold a standard-height Basic Box (see pages 12–13). Finish the bottom with a tab-lock insert or a side-to-side divider (see pages 19–22).

Folding a Lid or a Closed Box

Step 1: Complete Steps 1 through 7 of Flower Box II (pages 36–38). Use a measurement of 1½″ for the depth of the Sink Fold.

The width of the bands for this box will be twice the depth of the sink fold (d).

Step 2: Make the indicated valley folds. As you fold the flaps back, flatten the center multilayered square.

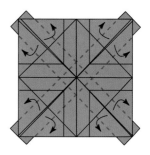

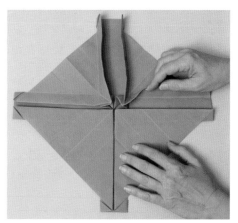

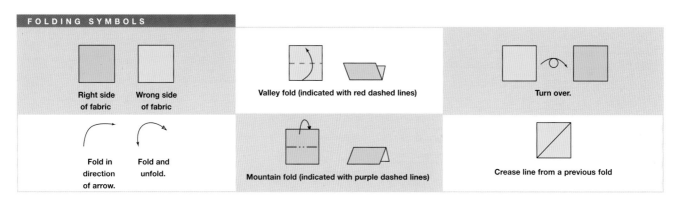

FOLDING SYMBOLS		
Right side of fabric / Wrong side of fabric	Valley fold (indicated with red dashed lines)	Turn over.
Fold in direction of arrow. / Fold and unfold.	Mountain fold (indicated with purple dashed lines)	Crease line from a previous fold

Fold back the flaps . . .

. . . and flatten.

Step 3: To fold a Self-Closing Box, follow the directions for the Self-Closing Box on pages 22–23, keeping the Victorian Box folds in place. Otherwise, follow the procedure for folding snugly fitting lids on pages 13–14.

Step 4: The inside flaps will interlock like they did for the Banded Box, or you can use a tab-lock insert (pages 19–20) to finish the box.

Step 5: Turn the lid over and shape the flower on the top.

Use tweezers to help shape the flower.

Size Options for Victorian Box Lids and Box Bottoms

	Starting Square (l)	Finished Height (h)	Finished Size (s)	Depth of Fold (d)
Lid	17″ × 17″	$1\frac{1}{2}$″	$6\frac{1}{4}$″ × $6\frac{1}{4}$″	$1\frac{3}{8}$″
Box Bottom	17″ × 17″	3″	6″ × 6″	
Lid	15″ × 15″	$1\frac{1}{4}$″	5″ × 5″	$1\frac{5}{8}$″
Box Bottom	15″ × 15″	3″	$4\frac{3}{4}$″ × $4\frac{3}{4}$″	
Lid	14″ × 14″	$1\frac{5}{8}$″	$4\frac{1}{4}$″ × $4\frac{1}{4}$″	$1\frac{1}{4}$″
Box Bottom	17″ × 17″	4″	4″ × 4″	
Lid	12″ × 12″	1″	$4\frac{1}{2}$″ × $4\frac{1}{2}$″	1″
Box Bottom	12″ × 12″	$2\frac{1}{8}$″ × $2\frac{1}{8}$″	$4\frac{1}{4}$″ × $4\frac{1}{4}$″	

Other Options

You can shape the ornament on the top of this box in several different ways. Pop the center up or let it lie flat.

The ornament on the top of this box has been popped up a lot. Notice the jewels and glitter paint highlights on this snowy purple snowflake box.

The ornament on the top of this box has been popped up just a little.

Fold some painted silk that is bonded to paper to make this simple but elegant box. Notice how the flower ornament has been shaped.

This fun plaid lies on the diagonal after the box is folded. This is a closed box, so you open it from the bottom.

Here's another way to form the flower on the top of the Victorian Box.

twisted square box I

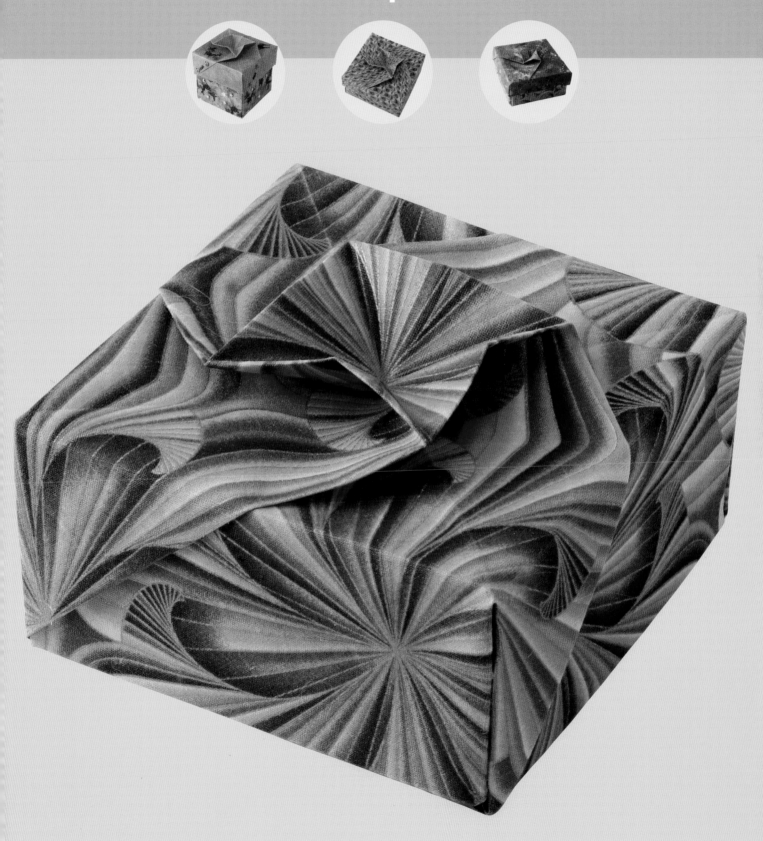

Have fun twisting a square on this box—the first of three twisted square boxes.

What You'll Need

Fabric

- For a Self-Closing Box: 1 fat quarter of stiffened fabric **OR**

- For a box and a lid: 2 fat quarters of stiffened fabric

- For a side-to-side divider for the box bottom: 1 fat quarter of stiffened fabric

Basic materials (See pages 5–7.)

Cutting the Fabric Squares

- For a Self-Closing Box: Cut 1 square 17″ × 17″ **OR**

- For a box and a lid: Cut 2 squares 17″ × 17″.

- For a tab-lock insert: Cut 2 smaller squares out of leftover fabric **OR**

- For a side-to-side divider: Cut 1 square 9½″ × 9½″.

Folding the Box Bottom

Fold a standard-height Basic Box (see pages 12–13). Finish the bottom with a tab-lock insert or a side-to-side divider (see pages 19–22).

Folding a Lid or a Closed Box

Step 1: With the wrong side of the square facing up, fold the fabric in half horizontally.

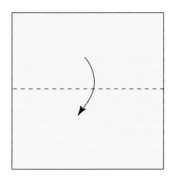

Step 2: Fold the piece in half vertically.

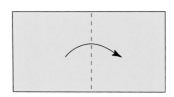

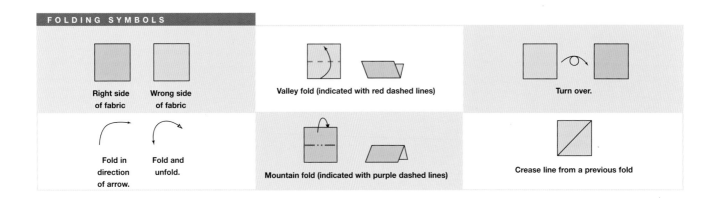

FOLDING SYMBOLS

| Right side of fabric | Wrong side of fabric |
| Valley fold (indicated with red dashed lines) |
| Turn over. |

| Fold in direction of arrow. | Fold and unfold. |
| Mountain fold (indicated with purple dashed lines) |
| Crease line from a previous fold |

Step 3: Be sure the folded edges are at the top and the cut edges are at the bottom. Make the indicated valley fold and unfold. The width of the folded section (*d*) is 1½".

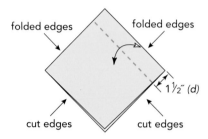

Step 4: Fold the top corner down. Unfold. The top point should lie on the fold line from Step 3.

Step 5: Fold and unfold the left edge. The arrow in the diagram below shows how the width is determined. The width of the fold section is the same as the fold in Step 3. Unfold completely.

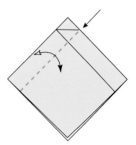

Step 6: Fold and unfold the indicated mountains and valleys. Pay particular attention to the purple mountain folds and the red valley fold in the center of the fabric square. Refold the horizontal mountain fold.

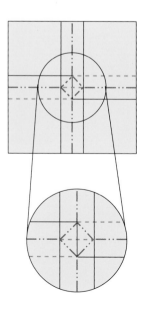

Step 7a: Form the mountain fold, shown in purple, that is perpendicular to the one made in Step 6. Be sure to make the mountain fold on the back as well. At the same time, push down on the valley fold line in the small center square.

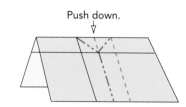

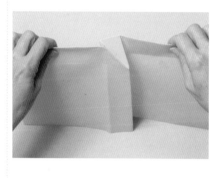

Step 7b: Fold the front rib that is formed to the right and the back rib to the left.

Step 8: Fold the top left rib forward and downward to form a twisted square.

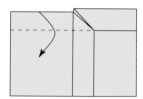

Step 9: Fold the back layer up.

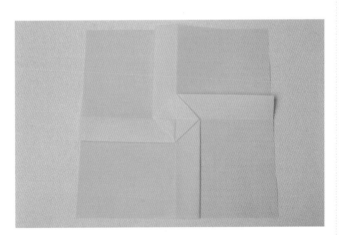

Step 10: To fold a Self-Closing Box, follow the directions for the Self-Closing Box on pages 22–23, keeping the Twisted Square folds in place. Otherwise, follow the procedure for folding snugly fitting lids on pages 13–14.

Step 11: Finish the inside of the lid with a tab-lock insert (pages 19–20).

Step 12: Turn the lid over and shape the twisted square on the top.

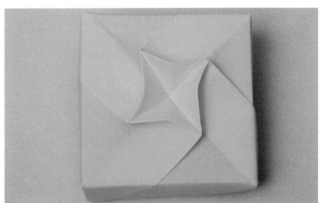

Size Options for Twisted Square Box I Lids and Box Bottoms

	Starting Square (*l*)	Finished Height (*h*)	Finished Size (*s*)	Depth of Fold (*d*)
Lid	$16^3/_4'' \times 16^3/_4''$	2"	5" × 5"	2"
Box Bottom	20" × 20"	$4^3/_4''$	$4^3/_4'' \times 4^3/_4''$	
Lid	15" × 15"	$1^1/_2''$	6" × 6"	$1^1/_4''$
Box Bottom	15" × 15"	$2^1/_2''$	$5^3/_4'' \times 5^3/_4''$	
Lid	14" × 14"	$1^1/_4''$	$5^1/_4'' \times 5^1/_4''$	$1^1/_2''$
Box Bottom	14" × 14"	$2^1/_2''$	5" × 5"	

Other Options

The square for this Halloween box was cut from a larger piece of fabric, not a fat quarter. You can make boxes as large as you want, but you will need to reinforce the sides of the box with cardboard. Notice the fabric cutouts on the lid.

To get the most out of this psychedelic pattern, we found one of the centers of the design and made it the center of the fabric square. Notice how the design radiates from the ornament.

A batik print and swirls make a very vibrant box.

twisted square box II

There's a double twist in this box, and the bands are more defined so the center ornament stands up higher on the box.

What You'll Need

Fabric

- For a Self-Closing Box: 1 fat quarter of stiffened fabric **OR**

- For a box and a lid: 2 fat quarters of stiffened fabric

- For a side-to-side divider for the box bottom: 1 fat quarter of stiffened fabric

Basic materials (See pages 5–7.)

Cutting the Fabric Squares

- For a Self-Closing Box: Cut 1 square 17″ × 17″ of stiffened fabric **OR**

- For a box and a lid: Cut 2 squares 17″ × 17″.

- For a tab-lock insert: Cut 2 smaller squares out of leftover fabric **OR**

- For a side-to-side divider: Cut 1 square 12½″ × 12½″.

Folding the Box Bottom

Fold a standard-height Basic Box (see pages 12–13). Finish the bottom with a tab-lock insert or a side-to-side divider (see pages 19–22).

Folding a Lid or a Closed Box

Step 1: Complete Steps 1 through 10 of Twisted Square Box I (see pages 46–48).

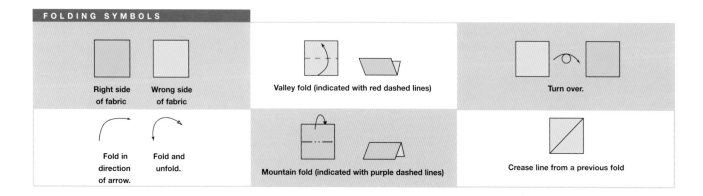

FOLDING SYMBOLS		
Right side of fabric / **Wrong side of fabric**	Valley fold (indicated with red dashed lines)	Turn over.
Fold in direction of arrow. / **Fold and unfold.**	Mountain fold (indicated with purple dashed lines)	Crease line from a previous fold

Step 2: Fold each rib toward the opposite side. As you fold each rib, you will be rotating the square one-quarter turn clockwise and making a new crease as shown in the photos.

After you finish Step 2, the center of your square should look like this.

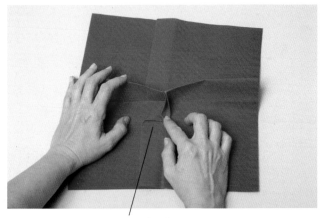

Look for right triangle

Step 3: Fold each rib in half lengthwise. Unfold the end of the rib near the center and refold, pushing the fold under the center square.

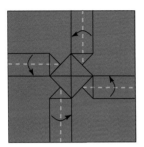

After you have folded all 4 ribs, the center of your square should look like this.

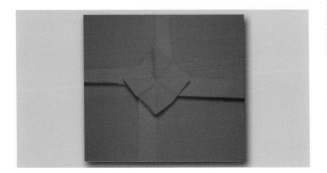

Step 4: To fold a Self-Closing Box, follow the directions for the Self-Closing Box on pages 22–23, keeping the Twisted Square folds in place. Otherwise, follow the procedure for folding snugly fitting lids on pages 13–14.

Step 5: Finish the inside of the lid with a tab-lock insert (pages 19–20).

Step 6: Turn the lid over and shape the twisted square on the top.

Size Options for Twisted Square Box II Lids and Box Bottoms

	Starting Square (l)	Finished Height (h)	Finished Size (s)	Depth of Fold (d)
Lid	17" × 17"	$1\frac{1}{2}$"	$6\frac{1}{4}$" × $6\frac{1}{4}$"	2"
Box Bottom	17" × 17"	3"	6" × 6"	
Box Insert	12" × 12"	$1\frac{3}{8}$"	$5\frac{7}{8}$" × $5\frac{7}{8}$"	
Divider	$8\frac{1}{4}$" × $8\frac{1}{4}$"			
Lid	$14\frac{1}{2}$" × $14\frac{1}{2}$"	$1\frac{1}{2}$"	$5\frac{1}{8}$" × $5\frac{1}{8}$"	$1\frac{1}{2}$"
Box Bottom	17" × 17"	$3\frac{1}{2}$"	5" × 5"	
Lid	16" × 16"	$1\frac{3}{4}$"	$5\frac{3}{4}$" × $5\frac{3}{4}$"	$1\frac{1}{2}$"
Box Bottom	16" × 16"	$2\frac{7}{8}$"	$5\frac{1}{2}$" × $5\frac{1}{2}$"	
Lid	17" × 17"	$1\frac{3}{8}$"	$6\frac{1}{4}$" × $6\frac{1}{4}$"	$2\frac{1}{8}$"
Box Bottom	17" × 17"	3"	6" × 6"	

Other Options

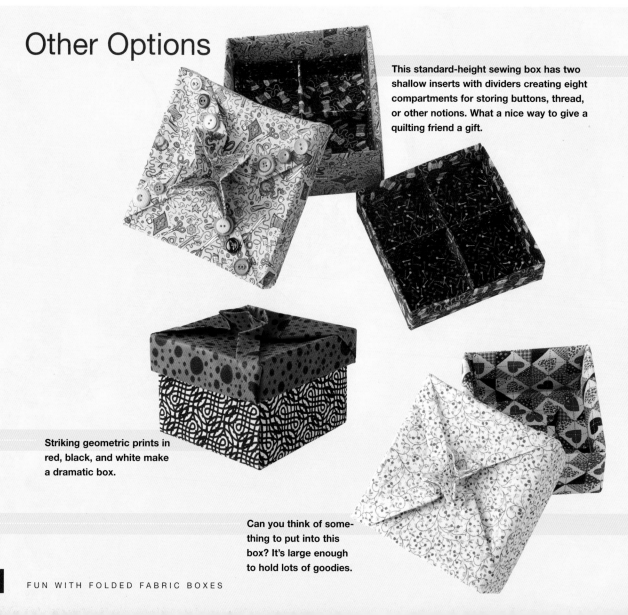

This standard-height sewing box has two shallow inserts with dividers creating eight compartments for storing buttons, thread, or other notions. What a nice way to give a quilting friend a gift.

Striking geometric prints in red, black, and white make a dramatic box.

Can you think of something to put into this box? It's large enough to hold lots of goodies.

twisted square box III

Cutting the Fabric Squares

- For a Self-Closing Box: Cut 1 square 17″ × 17″ of stiffened fabric **OR**

- For a box and a lid: Cut 2 squares 17″ × 17″.

- For a tab-lock insert: Cut 2 smaller squares out of leftover fabric **OR**

- For a side-to-side divider: Cut 1 square 12½″ × 12½″.

Here's one more twist to the Twisted Square Box. Notice the wider bands that cover the corners. Make several of these boxes to group together as a decorative accent.

What You'll Need

Fabric

- For a Self-Closing Box: 1 fat quarter of stiffened fabric **OR**

- For a box and a lid: 2 fat quarters of stiffened fabric

- For a side-to-side divider for the box bottom: 1 fat quarter of stiffened fabric

Basic materials (See pages 5–7.)

Folding the Box Bottom

Fold a standard-height Basic Box (see pages 12–13). Finish the bottom with a tab-lock insert or a side-to-side divider (see pages 19–22).

Folding a Lid or a Closed Box

Step 1: Complete Steps 1 through 3 of the Twisted Square Box II (see page 51–53).

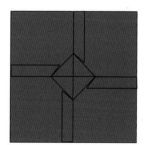

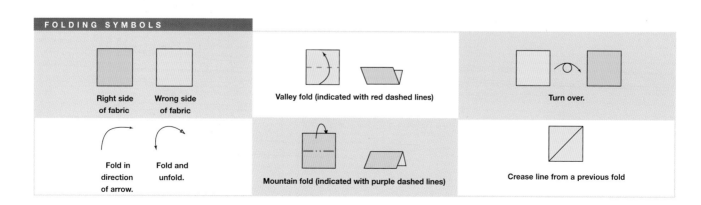

FOLDING SYMBOLS

Right side of fabric / Wrong side of fabric	Valley fold (indicated with red dashed lines)	Turn over.
Fold in direction of arrow. / Fold and unfold.	Mountain fold (indicated with purple dashed lines)	Crease line from a previous fold

Step 2: Unfold each rib, and stand it upright. Then flatten the rib, starting from the outside edge. At the center, tuck the flattened rib under the corner of the twisted square.

Step 3: To fold a Self-Closing Box, follow the directions for the Self-Closing Box on pages 22–23, keeping the Twisted Square folds in place. Otherwise, follow the procedure for folding snugly fitting lids on pages 13–14.

Step 4: Finish the inside of the lid with a tab-lock insert (pages 19–20).

Step 5: Turn the lid over and shape the twisted square on the top.

Size Options for Twisted Square Box III Lids and Box Bottoms

	Starting Square (l)	Finished Height (h)	Finished Size (s)	Depth of Fold (d)
Lid	17" × 17"	$1\frac{1}{4}$"	$6\frac{1}{4}$" × $6\frac{1}{4}$"	$2\frac{1}{4}$"
Box Bottom	17" × 17"	3"	6" × 6"	
Lid	15" × 15"	$1\frac{1}{4}$"	$5\frac{1}{8}$" × $5\frac{1}{8}$"	$2\frac{1}{4}$"
Box Bottom	16" × 16"	$3\frac{1}{4}$"	$4\frac{7}{8}$" × $4\frac{7}{8}$"	
Lid	15" × 15"	$1\frac{1}{4}$"	$6\frac{1}{2}$" × $6\frac{1}{2}$"	$1\frac{1}{4}$"
Box Bottom	15" × 15"	$2\frac{1}{4}$"	$6\frac{1}{4}$" × $6\frac{1}{4}$"	
Lid	14" × 14"	$1\frac{1}{4}$"	$4\frac{1}{4}$" × $4\frac{1}{4}$"	$2\frac{1}{4}$"
Box Bottom	14" × 14"	3"	4" × 4"	
Lid	12" × 12"	$1\frac{5}{8}$"	$3\frac{3}{4}$" × $3\frac{3}{4}$"	$1\frac{1}{8}$"
Box Bottom	15" × 15"	$3\frac{1}{2}$"	$3\frac{1}{2}$" × $3\frac{1}{2}$"	

Other Options

By changing the depth of the fold (d), you can vary the size of the ornament on the top of this box. Look at all the possibilities.

The pattern in this fabric is placed so that the diagonal bands stand out.

The elegant fabric used for the lid creates a very dramatic box.

The ornament on top of this tall box makes the box look even taller. The bronze bottom gives it a very elegant look.

This box has narrow bands and a small twisted square in the center. It would make a great container for a gift for a musical friend.

This shallow box is just the right size for a cheery springtime gift.

12″ square boxes

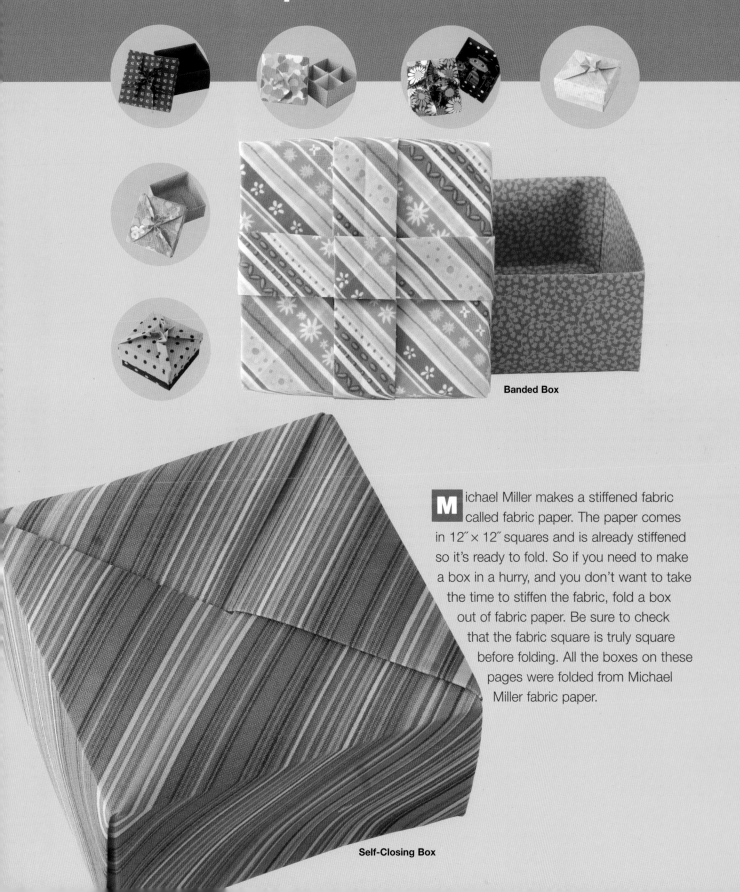

Banded Box

Michael Miller makes a stiffened fabric called fabric paper. The paper comes in 12″ × 12″ squares and is already stiffened so it's ready to fold. So if you need to make a box in a hurry, and you don't want to take the time to stiffen the fabric, fold a box out of fabric paper. Be sure to check that the fabric square is truly square before folding. All the boxes on these pages were folded from Michael Miller fabric paper.

Self-Closing Box

Flower Box II

Flower Box I

Victorian Box

Twisted Square Box I

Twisted Square Box II

Twisted Square Box III

How to Design a Box or Lid with Given Dimensions

Most of the boxes and decorative lids in this book are folded from fat quarters. You can fold larger boxes and lids out of larger pieces of fabric. You can use a "guess and check" approach to determine how large the starting square should be, or you can use the formulas listed below, which will provide approximate values for l, s, and h. The measurements of your box or lid will most likely be a little different than these values because of the weight of the fabric, the amount of stiffening, and the accuracy of your folding techniques.

l = edge length of the starting square for the bottom or lid

s = edge length of the square face of the bottom or lid

h = height of the bottom or overhang depth of the lid

d = depth of the fold that determines the size of the ornament on the box

w = width of the band on the lid

Box	Formula	Width of Band Formula
Basic Box	$l = 1.41 \times (s + 2h)$	
Banded Box	$l = 1.41 \times (s + 2d + 2h)$	$d = w$
Flower Box I	$l = 1.41 \times (s + d + 2h)$	$d = 1.41 \times w$
Flower Box II	$l = 1.41 \times (s + 2d + 2h)$	
Victorian Box	$l = 1.41 \times (s + 2d + 2h)$	$d = w/2$
Twisted Square Box I	$l = 1.41 \times (s + 1.41 \times d + 2h)$	
Twisted Square Box II	$l = 1.41 \times (s + 1.41 \times d + 2h)$	$d = 2w$
Twisted Square Box III	$l = 1.41 \times (s + 1.41 \times d + 2h)$	$d = w$

RESOURCES

fast2fuse Double-Sided Fusible Stiff Interfacing and Fabric Paper

Check your local quilt, fabric, or craft store or order from

C&T Publishing
800-284-1114
www.ctpub.com

The products listed below are available at fabric and craft stores and online.

Fabric Stiffeners

Stiffy Fabric Stiffener by Plaid Enterprises

Aleene's Fabric Stiffener and Draping Liquid

Spray Stiffeners

Aleene's Stiffen Quick

Stiffen Stuff Super Quick Stiffening Spray

Decoupage Finishes

Finishes and sealers are available in matte, glossy, and even sparkle.

Mod Podge

Amaco All-Purpose Sealer

For more information on origami folded boxes, including formulas that can be used as guides for the design of basic box and lid combinations, see *Unfolding Mathematics with Origami Boxes* by Arnold Tubis and Crystal Mills, published by Key Curriculum Press (Emeryville, CA, 2006).

For a list of other fine books from C&T Publishing, ask for a free catalog:

C&T Publishing, Inc.
P.O. Box 1456
Lafayette, CA 94549
800-284-1114
Email: ctinfo@ctpub.com
Website: www.ctpub.com

For quilting supplies:
Cotton Patch Mail Order
3405 Hall Lane, Dept. CTB
Lafayette, CA 94549
800-835-4418
925-283-7883
Email: quiltusa@yahoo.com
Website: www.quiltusa.com

Note: Fabrics used in the boxes shown may not be currently available as fabric manufacturers keep most fabrics in print for only a short time.

Crystal Mills lives in Blaine, Washington, which is at the northern end of Interstate 5, almost in Canada. She is a retired mathematics teacher and textbook editor. She loves to quilt and design wearable art. She became interested in origami when she was teaching high school mathematics. In her job as an editor, she edited an origami book, and after she retired, she co-authored *Unfolding Mathematics with Origami Boxes* with Arnold Tubis. Crystal and Arnold met at an origami convention in San Diego.

Crystal enjoys traveling and continues to present origami workshops for teachers throughout the country. She is looking forward to sharing her knowledge of origami with fabric enthusiasts.

Arnold Tubis received B.S. and Ph.D. degrees in physics from MIT. He was a member of the faculty of Purdue University from 1960 to 2000 (including nine years as a department head) and is the author or co-author of over a hundred research papers. He now lives in Carlsbad, California, where he is a visiting fellow at the University of California, San Diego in La Jolla and a consultant in the areas of auditory biophysics and the use of origami in K–12 mathematics education. He is currently working on a pilot origami-mathematics project in the Long Beach, California, school district. As an origami enthusiast since the early 1960s, Arnold has given many origami presentations and workshops focused on both the arts and mathematics, and has had his models on display in exhibitions in the United States, Europe, and Japan. His other interests include travel, playing the piano, and collecting and playing "strange" musical instruments.

Great Titles
from C&T PUBLISHING